INVADERS FROM EARTH

INVASIVE SPECIES IN THE AIR

Richard Spilsbury

PowerKiDS
press.

New York

Published in 2015 by The **Rosen Publishing Group**
29 East 21st Street, New York, NY 10010

Library of Congress Cataloging-in-Publication Data
Spilsbury, Richard, 1963- author.
 Invasive species in the air / Richard Spilsbury.
     pages cm. – (Invaders from Earth)
 Includes bibliographical references and index.
 ISBN 978-1-4994-0062-5 (pbk.)
 ISBN 978-1-4994-0031-1 (6 pack)
 ISBN 978-1-4994-0056-4 (library binding)
 1. Introduced birds–Juvenile literature. 2. Biological invasions–Juvenile literature.
 3. Environmental disasters–Juvenile literature. I. Title.
  QL677.79.I58S65 2015
  598.162–dc23
                                        2014027648

Produced for Rosen by Calcium
Editors for Calcium: Sarah Eason and Robyn Hardyman
Designer: Paul Myerscough

Photo credits: Cover: Shutterstock: Chris Hill; Inside: Dreamstime: Alessandrozocc
3, 6t, Archeophoto 16b, Viacheslav Belyaev 14bl, Musat Christian 25b, Gidejor
12b, Wael Hamdan 10b, Ron Hood 23t, Dusan Kostic 7, Brian Kushner 13t, Thomas
Langlands 6–7, Libux77 28, Makanature 8–9, Picstudio 15b, Inge Schepers 13b,
Pranay Sinha 21b, Radu Sporea 22–23, Thodsaph 28–29, Vasiliy Vishnevskiy 27t,
Wingkit 24–25, Wkruck 9t, Yadunandan 21t, Zhaozhonghua 4b; Shutterstock:
Georgios Alexandris 1, 24b, Florian Andronache 26b, Jez Bennett 12–13, Bildagentur
Zoonar GmbH 8b, Flaviano Fabrizi 10–11, Simon G 14br, J Gade 9c, Gallinago
Media 23c, Elliotte Rusty Harold 4–5, Chris Hill 18, Ronnie Howard 19b, Jadimages
19t, Alina Kurbiel 17, LJH Images 5t, Don Mammoser 25t, Mettus 11b, Mikeledray 27b,
M Lorenz 18–19, Targn Pleiades 6b, 22b, Paul Reeves Photography 5c, Huguette
Roe 29, Ruslanchik 14–15, S-F 11t, Dr Ajay Kumar Singh 20, Utopia_88 20–21, Herman
Veenendaal 16–17, Xpixel 26–27.

Manufactured in the United States of America
CPSIA Compliance Information: Batch CW15PK: For Further Information contact
Rosen Publishing, New York, New York at 1-800-237-9932

CONTENTS

WHAT ARE FLYING INVADERS?

An **invasive species** is one that is not **native** to an area and threatens it in some way. When birds from one place invade another, they may compete with native wildlife for resources such as food and space, kill off local insects or other animals, damage crops, and more!

Unwelcome Visitors

Birds can come to new places simply by flying there. They may be blown off course by the wind. Some are introduced by people who bring them as pets, or to sell, or control insect pests. Others come by accident, by getting trapped on a ship or an airplane.

CRANES

4

Increasing Invaders

Invader birds often thrive in new places because there are fewer **predators** and natural enemies to harm or kill them, or because they eat a wide variety of foods. This allows them to increase in number quickly and take over from local birds.

CANADA GEESE

Canada geese are native to North America but have spread as far as Europe, Australia, and parts of Asia and Russia.

EARTH UNDER ATTACK

Once they reach a new country, birds can spread more easily than some invaders because they can fly long distances, and cross rivers, lakes, and seas.

STARLING

European starlings are birds that have been introduced all over the world, usually because they are very pretty.
They are now considered a pest in most countries, because their enormous flocks make too much noise and produce huge amounts of waste.

FLOCK OF STARLINGS

Secrets of Success

Starlings spread easily because they eat almost anything, including insects, fruits, and seeds. They are also very **adaptable**. They can nest in a variety of places, from fields and marshes to garbage dumps and cities.

STARLINGS

Causing Damage

When a huge flock of starlings settles on a field or in an orchard, they damage plants that grow there. They eat fruit crops such as cherries and pull up young grain plants to eat the seeds. They are aggressive birds, so they also threaten native birds by taking their food and their nesting spaces.

Some flocks of starlings are made up of thousands of birds. They cause crop damage each year that is valued at hundreds of millions of dollars.

INVADER ANALYSIS

A popular story is that 100 starlings were released in Central Park, New York, in 1890. Since then the starling population in the United States has grown to around 150 million!

MUTE SWAN

Mute swans are large, beautiful birds that can fly long distances. This means they sometimes end up in places where their big appetites and aggressive behavior disrupt the local wildlife.

Greedy Birds

Mute swans use their long necks to reach the underwater plants that they eat. In some places they eat so much that they kill off the plants there. This reduces the amount of food for other water birds and affects local **food chains**. The swans' feeding also churns up mud, making the water too cloudy for some fish.

MUTE SWAN

SWANS' NEST

Snapping Swans

Mute swans get very aggressive when other animals come near their nests. They will chase off native ducks, swans, and other water birds. They sometimes even attack and kill them.

EARTH UNDER ATTACK

Occasionally, mute swans attack people on boats and on shore if they enter the swans' **territory**. Mute swans have large, heavy bills and can bite hard and cause injury, so keep your distance!

ROCK DOVE

In cities around the world, people enjoy watching and feeding rock doves, or pigeons as they are also called. However, these increasingly familiar birds can be a big nuisance.

In Your Neighborhood

Rock doves are native to Europe. They were introduced to the United States and the rest of the world to be reared for food. Escaped rock doves spread when they started **breeding**. Rock doves usually settle near farmland or farm buildings, where they eat insects, seeds, and people's leftovers. In the country, they eat and **contaminate** large food stores that are meant for people or livestock.

ROCK DOVE

INVADER ANALYSIS

Rock doves cause $1.1 billion worth of damage in US cities every year.

Droppings and Disease

Rock dove droppings are **corrosive**. In cities, large amounts of them damage buildings and monuments, kill plants, and give off an unpleasant smell. Rock doves can also pass on diseases such as salmonella. Their nests are infested with ticks, fleas, and mites, which can cause health problems, too. These birds even cause problems around airports, where they sometimes fly into aircraft.

CITY BIRD

Rock doves in cities often feed on food in trash cans or that people drop on the street.

11

CATTLE EGRET

Cattle egrets are also known as elephant birds and hippopotamus egrets, because they are often seen on the backs of these large mammals. They feed on ticks on their skin and on small animals that the elephants and hippopotamus disturb as they eat.

Global Grazers

Cattle egrets are native to Africa but now live worldwide. After flying across the Atlantic from Africa, they spread from South America to the United States in just 50 years. Now they are one of the most common US herons, all the way to Alaska.

In Africa, cattle egrets often hitch a ride on zebras as well as cattle.

CATCHING DINNER

CATTLE EGRET

Good and Bad

Some farmers welcome cattle egrets because they remove blood-sucking ticks from their livestock. Ticks can make animals weak or sick. However, young ticks simply hitch a ride on the egrets to the next animals they land on.

INVADER ANALYSIS

Cattle egrets nest in trees by water. A male and female pair rear up to five young egrets. Six weeks after hatching, the young birds begin to fly. They may then fly up to 3,000 miles (4,830 km) away from where they started life.

COMMON MYNA

The common myna was introduced to Australia, Hawaii, and other places to feed on insect pests that threaten crops. It is native to India. Unfortunately, it causes so much damage in its new homes that it is now regarded as a pest!

People Problems

Mynas gather together in flocks of many thousands. In cities, their constant, noisy chattering is a problem, and their droppings can pass on diseases. Flocks of mynas also damage fruit crops because they eat so many berries, fruits, and seeds.

MYNA FLOCK

MYNAS ON A WILDEBEEST

Wildlife Worries

Mynas also harm **indigenous** wildlife. They threaten small mammals and birds by taking over their nesting sites. On some islands, such as Hawaii and Fiji, they threaten other bird species by eating their eggs and chicks.

Mynas are sometimes bought as pets. Escaped pet mynas may breed and invade new areas.

EARTH UNDER ATTACK

Several bird species are in danger of **extinction** because of mynas. The Mauritius parakeet almost died out after mynas stole its nesting sites. In Australia, mynas are threatening the superb parrot in the same way, so that only a few thousand are now left.

15

RUDDY DUCK

The ruddy duck is a US bird that was introduced into the United Kingdom in the 1940s. Some birds escaped and bred, creating successful wild populations. When ruddy ducks flew to and settled in Spain, they became a real threat to the country's native rare white-headed duck.

Harmful Hybrids

Ruddy ducks are killing off white-headed ducks by breeding with them. They produce ducklings that are part ruddy duck, part white-headed duck. Over time, hybrids mate with more ruddy ducks and any white-headed duck features eventually disappear.

Ruddy ducks could cause the extinction of white-headed ducks like these.

16

Ruddy Control

Ruddy ducks are common in their native North America where they number more than half a million. In Europe, ruddy ducks are much rarer because they are legally hunted.

RUDDY DUCK

INVADER ANALYSIS

There are fewer than 10,000 white-headed ducks in the whole world. Around 2,500 of these are in Spain. This population is only just recovering from near extinction in the 1970s, caused by habitat loss and hunting.

GREAT HORNED OWL

Great horned owls have huge eyes that are fixed in their sockets. To look around, the birds twist their head nearly all the way around!

With giant yellow eyes surrounded by orange feathers and tufts that look like horns, the great horned owl's face is unmistakable. The owl is many small animals' worst nightmare!

INVADER ANALYSIS

The great horned owl has amazing eyesight and can see prey even in low light. If this owl was the same size as a human, its eyes would be the size of grapefruit! Its ears are hidden behind feathers around the eyes, and they can hear a mouse squeaking 900 feet (274 m) away.

Top Predators

Great horned owls are fierce **nocturnal** predators. They are big enough to capture and kill anything from Canada geese to skunks. They are not fussy eaters and will find something to eat wherever they live, from the Arctic to warm grasslands.

GREAT HORNED OWL

Rat Killers?

In the 1920s, the government of French Polynesia introduced great horned owls to hunt rats that were damaging the country's crops. Sadly, the owls had little effect on the rat population but killed off rare native birds such as the Marquesan imperial pigeon.

GREAT HORNED OWL CHICKS

19

RED-VENTED BULBUL

The red-vented
bulbul often nests
in strange places
inside buildings,
so people think it
first spread from
southern Asia after
nesting inside a
container on a
ship! Since then, it has spread to
the United States, New Zealand,
and Pacific islands from pet birds
that escaped from their cages.

RED-VENTED BULBUL

Breeding Bulbuls

The red-vented bulbul spreads quickly
because it nests in a wide range of
places, and because females can lay up
to three sets of eggs every year. Each
set usually contains two to five eggs.

This is one of the worst invasive alien bird species in the world.

Spreading Trouble

The red-vented bulbul reduces native bird species by chasing them off nesting sites and competing for food. It is a pest in farms and backyards because it eats fruit, flowers, and beans. It also spreads invasive plant species by eating their fruits and spreading the seeds in its droppings.

FRUIT EATER

EARTH UNDER ATTACK

In 2014, the New Zealand government offered a reward of $1,000 for a red-vented bulbul sighting that led to the successful capture and removal of this invasive, unwanted bird.

21

MALLARD

If you glance at your nearest duck pond, you will likely see a mallard. This handsome duck is the most common and widely distributed of all ducks on Earth. However, its success has come at a cost to other ducks.

Getting Around

Mallards historically come from the Northern Hemisphere. Some have invaded naturally by flying in. Others have been introduced by people for hunting, as useful farm animals, or even as pets because of their beautiful feathers.

FEMALE MALLARD WITH DUCKLINGS

Mallard Mayhem

Mallards breed with other ducks to create hybrids. The gray duck in New Zealand and yellow-billed duck in Africa are threatened species because of this. Mallards also pass on a virus through their droppings that causes a disease called bird flu. Bird flu spreads among birds but can affect humans, too.

A FLOCK OF MALLARDS

INVADER ANALYSIS

There are around 30 million mallards worldwide. The duck is considered a native species everywhere from Australia to Yemen. Almost all domestic ducks (ducks raised for their feathers or their meat) are related to the mallard.

A male mallard has a shiny green head. The female has pretty, mottled-brown feathers.

ROSE-RINGED PARAKEET

This colorful, distinctive bird is native to central Africa and Asia but now breeds in over 35 countries. In fact, it is one of the most successful bird invaders in the world.

Success Story

Rose-ringed parakeets spread after caged birds escaped. Although they come from warm, tropical places, they cope well with cold winters in places such as the United Kingdom. They also succeed because they eat many types of food, including berries, nuts, seeds, and household scraps.

ROSE-RINGED PARAKEET FEEDING

Rose-ringed parakeets are a serious problem for farmers and fruit growers because they are such wasteful feeders. They tend to take one or two pecks from each fruit and then move on to the next. As a result, one bird can damage many plants.

ROSE-RINGED PARAKEET NEST

Parakeet Problems

The problem with rose-ringed parakeets is that they compete with native bird species, such as woodpeckers and nuthatches, for nest holes. They also feed on and damage crops such as fruit trees and grape vines.

Parakeets are beautiful, but they are also destructive!

25

HOUSE SPARROW

Sparrows were introduced to the United States from Europe in the 1850s. They were brought to the United States by settlers who wanted to have birds from their home countries and by farmers who wanted to use the birds to control agricultural pests.

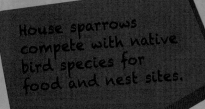

House sparrows compete with native bird species for food and nest sites.

House to Home

The house sparrow did not have any natural predators when it arrived in the United States, so it soon spread. The bird eats a wide range of food, from seeds and spiders to food scraps. It also nests near people, where there is a plentiful food supply, such as on barns or houses.

Nest Theft

House sparrows do eat insect pests such as cotton caterpillars, but they are more likely to damage grain crops and steal food meant for farm birds. They scare other birds off their nests, and sometimes even break their eggs and kill chicks. They even kill adult birds. They are a threat to native birds such as purple martins, the Carolina wren, and some woodpeckers.

A FLOCK OF SPARROWS

SPARROW'S NEST

INVADER ANALYSIS

Between 1850 and 1881, around 1,600 sparrows were brought to the United States from England. They bred fast and populations grew. In fact, at one time there were so many that sparrows were sold in markets as food!

NEW INVASIONS

Increases in trade and travel, and in the sale of exotic pets, mean there are likely to be more bird invaders in the future. What can we do to stop them harming habitats and native species?

Government Action

Governments make laws about the types of pets that can be brought into a country. When a bird invader causes serious problems, the authorities hire people to capture and remove them. In some cases, such as ruddy ducks, they even kill large numbers of birds.

BIRD SCARER

Governments need to encourage people to reduce waste. Waste attracts invasive species such as these gulls, which are searching for food on a landfill site.

How You Can Help

People can help by putting up bird nesting boxes that suit native birds. It is also important that people never release exotic and pet birds into the wild. If they no longer wish to keep their pets, they should take them to a local rescue organization or pet store instead.

EARTH UNDER ATTACK

Many scientists believe that the Earth is getting warmer and experiencing more extreme weather events. This could cause birds that usually live in warmer places to spread to places that were once too cold for them.

GLOSSARY

adaptable Adjusts to new situations.

breed To make young or babies.

contaminate To pollute.

corrosive Able to damage metal and stone.

extinction The dying out of a plant or animal.

food chain A way of showing how energy is passed from one living thing to another.

habitat A place where plants or animals live.

indigenous Born in or belonging to a particular place.

invasive species A kind of plant or animal not native to an area and causing it harm.

native Born in or belonging to a particular place.

nocturnal Active mainly during the night.

predators Animals that hunt and eat other animals.

prey An animal that is hunted and eaten by other animals.

territory The area that an animal lives in and defends.

virus A tiny living thing that causes disease.

FURTHER READING

Books

Alderfer, Jonathan. *National Geographic Kids Bird Guide of North America: The Best Birding Book for Kids from National Geographic's Bird Experts*. Des Moines, IA: National Geographic Children's Books, 2013.

Hartman, Eve, and Wendy Meshbesher. *What Is the Threat of Invasive Species?* (Sci-Hi: Science Issues). North Mankato, MN: Capstone, 2012.

Heinrichs Gray, Susan. *Starling* (Animal Invaders). North Mankato, MN: Cherry Lake Publishing, 2008.

Websites

Due to the changing nature of Internet links, PowerKids Press has developed an online list of websites related to the subject of this book. This site is updated regularly. Please use this link to access the list:
www.powerkidslinks.com/ife/air

INDEX